The

SEDER
ACTIVITY
Book

by Judy Dick

UAHC Press

New York, New York

This book is printed on acid-free paper.

Copyright © 2001 by Judy Dick

Manufactured in the United States of America

10 9 8 7 6 5 4 3 2 1

Welcome to
The Seder Activity Book

This book is a great way to prepare for Passover. You can also use this book during the seder itself.

The word *seder* means "order." Did you know that there are fourteen steps to the Passover seder? This book takes you through all fourteen steps, from the beginning of the seder to the end. The big Seder Time Clock on pages 10-11 shows you all fourteen steps, in the correct order. The clock that appears on some of the pages of this book tells you where you are in the fourteen steps.

Have a great time using this book, and enjoy your seder, all fourteen steps of it!

You Are Invited

To a SEDER,
the festive Passover meal!

WHEN: _____

WHO: _____

WHERE: _____

_____

RSVP: _____

WELCOME

Fill in the invitation. To make invitations to send to others, trace the dark lines and words. Design your own frame, fill in the information, cut out the shape, and send it to your friends!

SEDER JUMBLE

At the Seder we use many objects that help us celebrate Passover. The Passover objects below are waiting for the seder to begin. They are all mixed up! Prepare for the seder by sorting and coloring them.

- Find **matzot** and **circle them** in **red.**
  Hint: "Matzot" is the plural for "matzah."

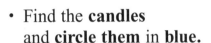

- Find the **candles** and **circle them** in **blue.**

- Find the **Cup of Elijah** and **circle it** in **purple.**

- Find the **cups** and **circle them** in **yellow.**

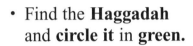

- Find the **Haggadah** and **circle it** in **green.**

- Find the **6 foods of the seder plate** and **circle them** in **orange.**
  Find these foods below by unscrambling their names. They are *BEITZAH, Z'ROA, MAROR, CHAROSET, CHAZERET* and *KARPAS.*

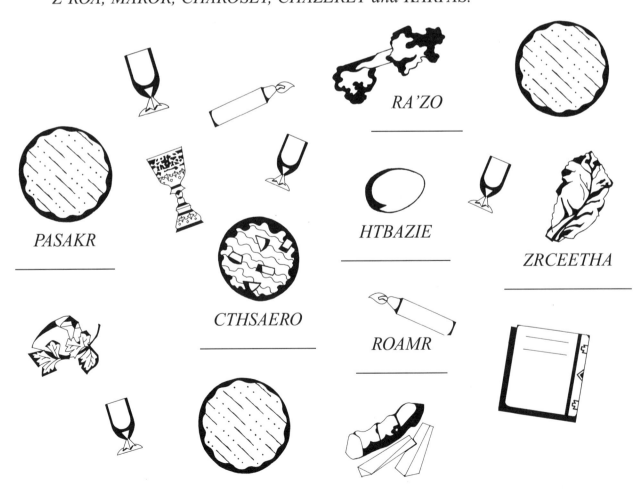

RA'ZO

PASAKR

HTBAZIE

ZRCEETHA

CTHSAERO

ROAMR

PASSOVER NUMBERS

Now that you have found all the Passover objects, can you count them? Look back at page 6 to fill in the answers below.

I came to the seder and I saw:

Numbers:

_____   We drink _____ cups of wine at the seder.

_____   We eat _____ matzot, Passover bread, at the seder.

_____   We light _____ candles to give us light at the seder.

_____   At the seder, we read from the Haggadah, the book that teaches us Passover stories and customs. Everyone gets a Haggadah to read from. How many would your family use? _____

_____   We pour _____ Cup of Elijah.

_____   We place _____ foods on the seder plate.

Write the name of each food on the line below it.

1.

_____

2.

_____

3.

_____

4.

_____

5.

_____

6.

_____

SEDER SETUP

Now you are ready to set the table for the seder.

קְעָרָה

K'ARAH

BEITZAH

Z'ROA

MAROR

KARPAS

CHAROSET

CHAZERET

Some seder plates hold their dishes on top and **matzot** below on shelves. Draw the foods of the seder plate on the dishes with their names. (For help, look at pages 6 and 7. Next draw in one more **matzah** on the shelf below the other two.

Color the whole page in honor of the seder!

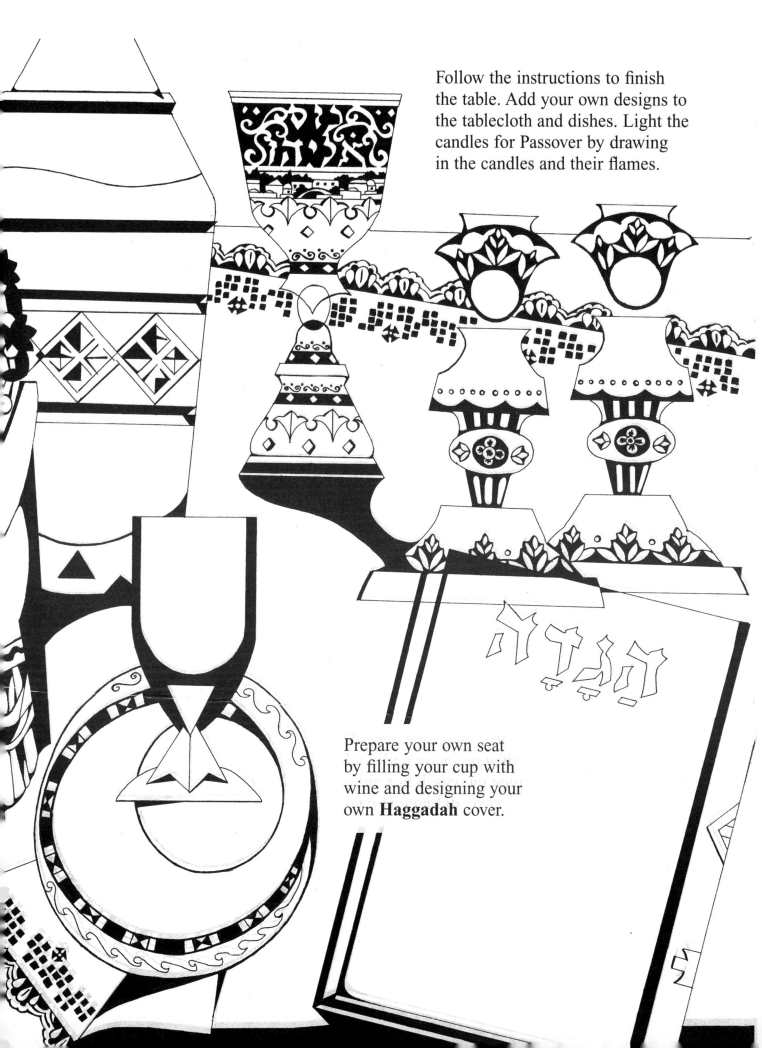

Follow the instructions to finish the table. Add your own designs to the tablecloth and dishes. Light the candles for Passover by drawing in the candles and their flames.

Prepare your own seat by filling your cup with wine and designing your own **Haggadah** cover.

The scene is set. When do we begin?
Color in three stars, and the
night can start!

KADEISH

URCHAT

NIRTZAH

HALLEL

1

14

13

BAREICH

10

SEDER TIME

The seder has its own timetable. It has 14 steps that each have their own name. Follow the numbers to learn their names.

KARPAS — 3

YACHATZ — 4

MAGGID — 5

RACHTZAH — 6

MATZAH MOTZI — 7

MAROR — 8

KORECH — 9

SHULCHAN OREICH — 10

TZAFUN — 11

Passover always falls in the same season. Which season is it? _____ Find the answer in the clock. Then find the birds, butterflies, and flowers in the clock. Color them in to show everyone the time of year. Why do you think Passover falls in this season?

Watch for the clock later in the book to know what time of the seder you are in.

Seder Menu

Food is an important and tasty part of the seder. There are a number of dishes at the seder table that remind us of life in Egypt before we were freed from slavery and of the original Passover in Egypt.

To learn about tonight's menu, read the rebus and fill in the blanks by choosing adjectives from the box below that describe each dish.

Chef's Specialities

All dishes are served with 4  of _____ .

MATZAH: Passover bread that is _____ and _____ .

CHAROSET: A _____ made **2** look like the clay the Jews used to make bricks with in Egypt. **2-** 's ch*aroset* is made from , , and cinnamon.

MAROR: UR choice of - or Romaine . Both will help **U** remember the _____ life of our ancestors as in Egypt.

BEITZAH: This sits uneaten **2** remind us of the Festival sacrifice eaten in the Temple in Jerusalem many years ago.

Z'ROA: _____ meat that reminds us of the Passover sacrifice eaten in the Temple in Jerusalem many years ago.

KARPAS: Delicious vegetables served dipped in . **UR** choice of or _____ parsley.

HILLEL SANDWICH: The chef's favorite, a tasty combination of , *maror,* and *charoset.*

green roasted sweet bitter dry red crispy

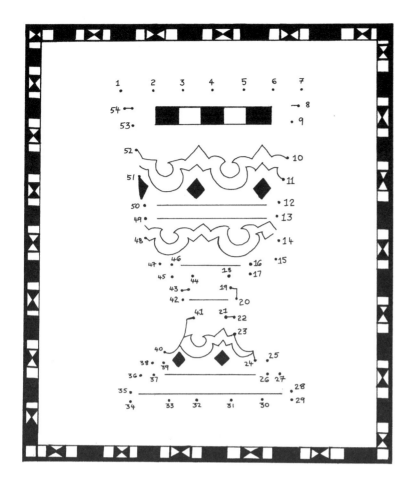

The table is set, the time is right —
let the seder begin!

On seder night we do many activities. Discover the actions we do and with which objects by completing the dot-to-dot pictures. Then fill in the blanks with the answers.

(For extra help, unscramble the clues.)

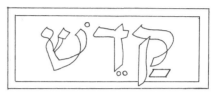

1

KADEISH

We say **Kiddush,** a blessing over the

_____. (EWIN)

We use a _____ _____

(DDKIHSU PCU), the first one of the night!

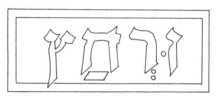

2

URCHATZ

Next we _____ _____ _____.
(AWSH ORU SHDAN)

We use a

_____.

(AWGNSHI PUC)

13

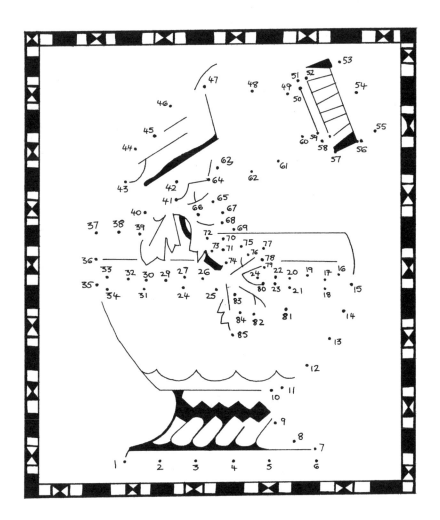

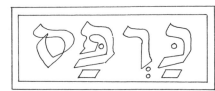

3

KARPAS

We take the vegetables for Karpas,

perhaps some _____
(EYPSALR)

Then we _____ (PDI)
them in _____

_____

(LSAT TRAWE) and eat them.

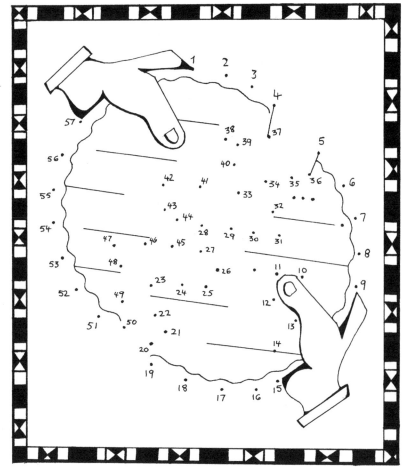

4

YACHATZ

The seder leader takes the

_____ and
(AZMATH)

_____ (KEBRAS)

it into 2 pieces. One half is returned
to its place and the other is saved for
the AFIKOMAN.

MAGGID

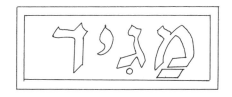

Now we take the and learn about the meaning of Passover.
Do you know what Haggadah means?

We are taught by our sages to learn the Passover story by discussing it.

This includes asking many questions! The even starts us off with four
questions, called the *MAH NISHTANAH.*

1. Why tonight do we eat
_____ ?

4. Why tonight do we
_____ ?

MAH NISHTANAH:
How is this night different from all other nights?

Finish the 4 questions by looking at the people who ask
them. What is each one doing?

2. Why tonight do we eat _____ ?

3. Why tonight do we
_____ twice?

Answer: Haggadah, related to the word *Maggid,* means "telling over." The Haggadah retells the Passover story.

Each section contains a hidden clue about one stage of the early history of the Jewish people. Write the clue in the space provided. Then discover the main mitzvah by filling in the circled letters in the spaces below.

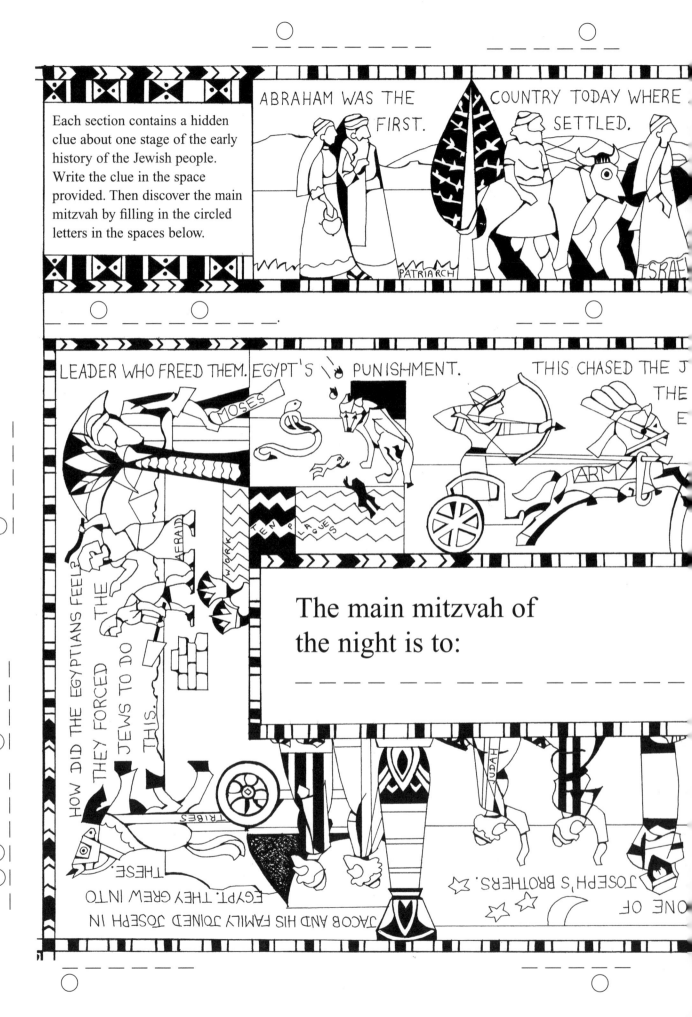

ABRAHAM WAS THE FIRST.

COUNTRY TODAY WHERE SETTLED.

PATRIARCH

ISRAEL

LEADER WHO FREED THEM.

EGYPT'S PUNISHMENT.

THIS CHASED THE J THE E

MOSES

TEN PLAGUE

ARMY

HOW DID THE EGYPTIANS FEEL THEY FORCED THE JEWS TO DO THIS.

AFRAID

WORK

The main mitzvah of the night is to:

_ _ _ _ _ _ _ _ _ _ _ _ _ _ _

JUDAH

TRIBES

THESE

JACOB AND HIS FAMILY JOINED JOSEPH IN EGYPT. THEY GREW INTO

ONE OF JOSEPH'S BROTHERS.

The Egyptians wrote in hieroglyphs, also called picture writing. Imagine that you found an ancient Egyptian scroll that told of the Ten Plagues! Use the code below to decipher the hieroglyphs on the next page and learn their names. Fill in the letter for each picture. Then color the pages.

Ten

1.

2.

3.

4.

5.

6.

7.

8.

9.

10.

(Check your answers on page 35)

Rabban Gamliel, a talmudic sage, taught that it is important for us to explain the meaning of three things on seder night. Which three things do you think he meant? (Look at the pictures and fill in the name of each object below its Hebrew name.)

Each of these objects reminds us of our past in Egypt. Using the color code below, find out about this past by coloring in the hidden pictures. What can you see? Now complete Rabban Gamliel's explanations for each symbol.

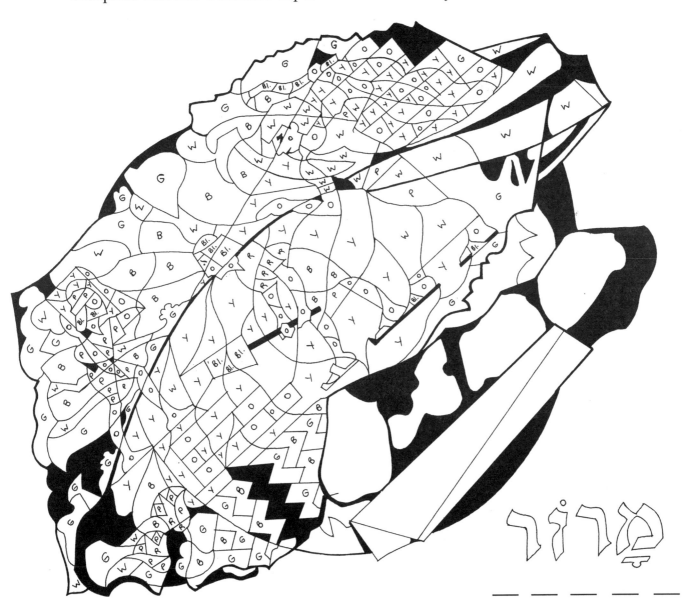

מָרוֹר

___ ___ ___ ___ ___

3. This reminds us of the bitter life we led in

_____ when we were _____.

COLOR CODE			
Y = yellow	**B** = blue	**R** = red	**Bl.** = Black
O = orange	**G** = green	**P** = purple	**W** = white

פֶּסַח

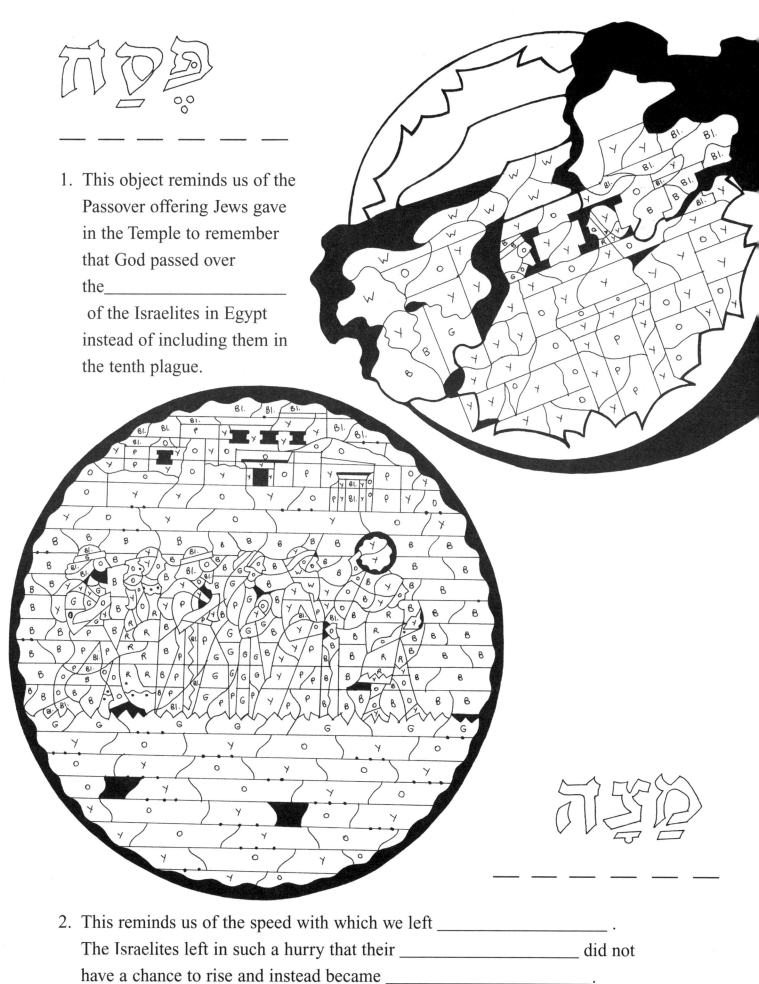

1. This object reminds us of the Passover offering Jews gave in the Temple to remember that God passed over the _____ of the Israelites in Egypt instead of including them in the tenth plague.

מַצָּה

_ _ _ _ _ _ _

2. This reminds us of the speed with which we left _____ . The Israelites left in such a hurry that their _____ did not have a chance to rise and instead became _____ .

(Check your answers on page 35)

The Passover story and the seder activities help us to remember what it was like to be slaves in Egypt and then be freed.

We lean and drink wine to feel like free people.

Draw in the expressions on the people leaning back in their chairs. What does it feel like to be free?

Then turn the page around and remember the slavery in Egypt. We eat matzah and *maror* to feel like slaves in Egypt. What might it have felt like? Draw in expressions for the Jews in slavery.

Color both sides. What colors do you think show freedom? What colors show slavery?

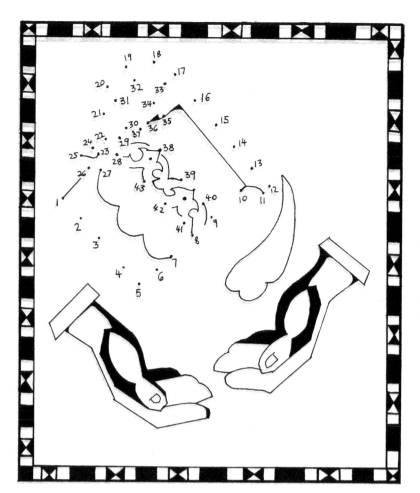

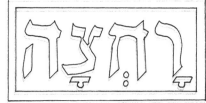

RACHTZAH

We _____
our hands before eating
the matzah.

MOTZI MATZAH

We say a blessing over
the _____
and then _____ it!

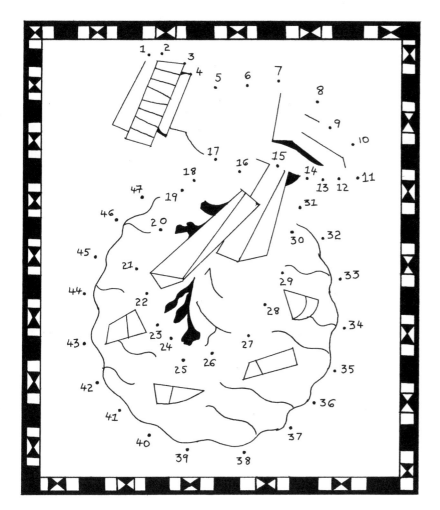

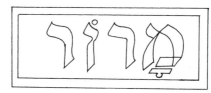

MAROR

We _____ the

_____ in

_____, say

a blessing, and

_____ it.

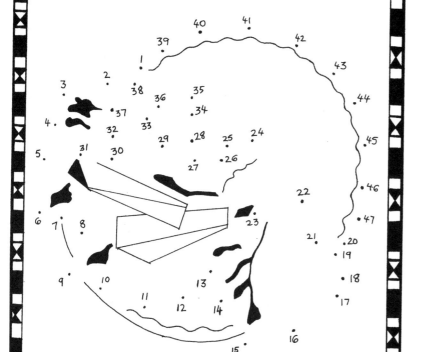

KORECH

We take some

_____

and _____

and put them together to
make a "Hillel Sandwich."
Hillel was a sage who
began this tradition in the
times of the Temple.
We drink the second cup
of wine

(Check your answers on page 35)   25

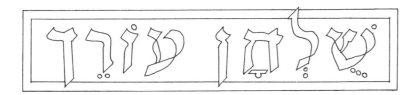

SHULCHAN OREICH

After learning about and discussing Passover, we are ready to eat the meal! What would you like to eat? Draw your favorite Passover foods on the plate below. Then make it look even more delicious by coloring it in.

On Passover we do not eat *chametz*.

Chametz is _____.

Circle the foods below that are not *chametz*.

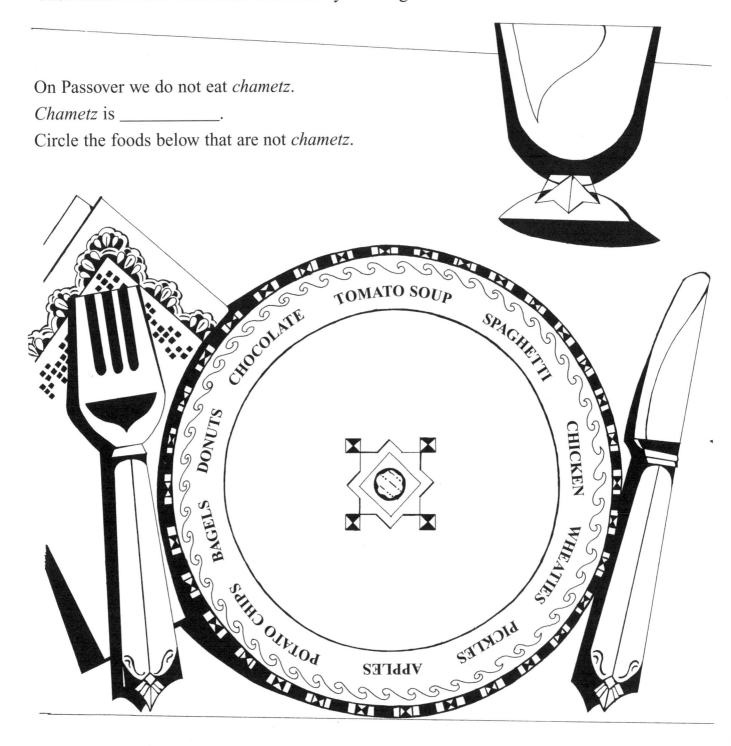

TOMATO SOUP · CHOCOLATE · SPAGHETTI · DONUTS · CHICKEN · BAGELS · WHEATIES · POTATO CHIPS · APPLES · PICKLES

TZAFUN

One meaning for *tzafun* is "hidden." Do you remember what some people hide, at the beginning of the seder? (Hint: Look under *Yachatz.*) It now becomes dessert, the last thing we eat at the seder table.

ANSWER: __ __ __ __ __ __ __ __

11

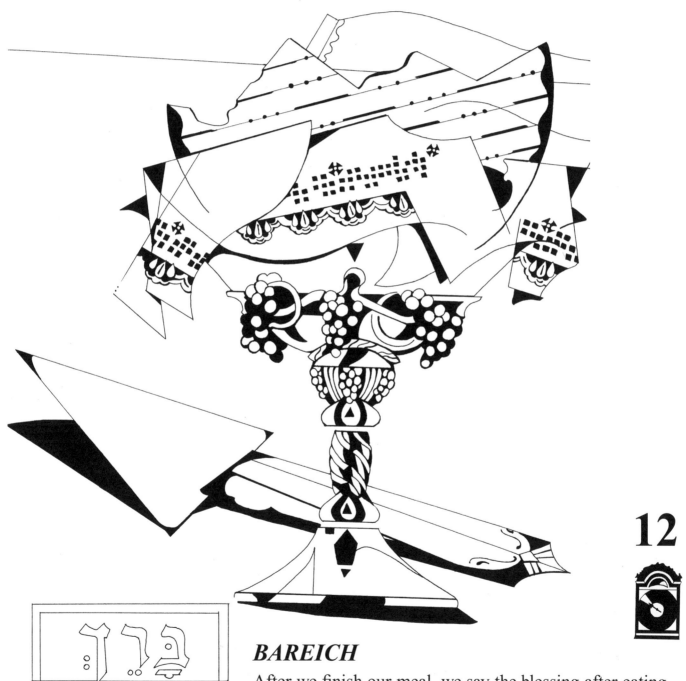

12

BAREICH

After we finish our meal, we say the blessing after eating .

(Check your answers on page 35)

We drink cup number 3 and pour cup number 4.

We fill the Cup of Elijah with wine. Many families open the front door at this time. What reasons can you think of for this custom?

HALLEL

We sing songs of praise to God expressing our thanks for the miracles of the past and hope for the future.

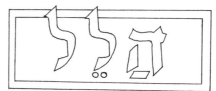

We drink cup number 4.

We have drunk 4 cups at the seder. One reason we drink 4 cups is because the Torah lists 4 words of freedom. Can you find these Hebrew words in the 4 cups below?

Jerusalem

יְרוּשָׁלַיִם

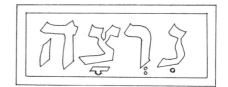

NIRTZAH

The Passover seder has come to an end. We
hope that this will be a year of peace
for everyone. We say:

Next year in Jerusalem

Help everyone from the 4 corners of the
world make their way to Jerusalem in time
to enjoy the next Passover together!

We end the seder with **Chad Gadya,** "One Little Goat," a song that has been sung at seders for hundreds of years.

This little goat is the start of a whole chain of events! Follow the chain by connecting the dot-to-dots.

Then came the Holy One and removed the angel of death.

10.

Then came a cat and ate the goat.

2.

9.

Then came the angel of death and took away the butcher.

1.

1 little goat, one little goat, that father bought for **2** zuzim.

Then came a dog and bit the cat.

3.

8.

Then came the butcher and slaughtered the ox.

Then came a stick and beat the dog.

4.

7.

6.

Then came water and put out the fire.

5.

Then came fire and burned the stick.

Then came an ox and drank the water.

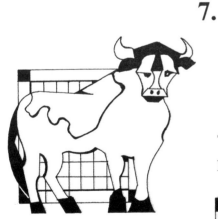

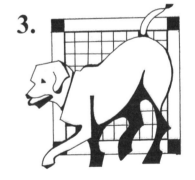

Congratulations on completing the seder! Can you remember everything that happened? If you can, this last activity will be a snap!

Fill in the names of the seder times next to the correct symbol and finish on top!

1 *Example*
<u>K A D E I S H</u>

(Check your answers on page 35)

33

Answers

The hidden words are in capital letters, and the circled letters are in bold. Check your answers below.

Abraham was the first PA**T**RIARCH and Sarah was the first matriarch.

The country where Abraham settled later became known as ISRA**E**L.

A place in ancient Canaan was BEIT **E**L.

Abraham's nephew was named **L**OT.

A child that is a boy is a S**O**N.

Rebecca, to Isaac, was his WI**F**E.

Jacob and Esau were **T**WINS.

What was Esau? He was said to be a **H**UNTER.

Where did Jacob study? According to legend, Jacob studied in his T**E**NT.

The number of Jacob's children is THIRTEEN.

How many with Leah? They had SI**X** sons.

Jacob's favorite son, who was sold into slavery, was **J**OSEPH.

Joseph explained **D**REAMS, which led him to become second-in-command to Pharoah.

One of Joseph's brothers was **J**UDAH.

Jacob and his family joined Joseph in Egypt. They grew into the twelve TRIBE**S**.

How did the Egyptians feel? They were A**F**R**A**ID that the Jews were growing too numerous.

They forced the Jews to W**O**RK for them as slaves.

The leader who freed the Jews was **M**OSES.

Egypt's punishment for their cruelty to the Jews was the TEN PLAGUES.

The Egyptian AR**M**Y chased the Jews as they left Egypt.

God **S**PLIT the sea and then the Jews were free.

In pain, they let the Jews leave, but at the last moment Pharoah changed his mind. He led his ARMY in chasing after them.

The Egyptians caught up to the Jewish nation as they faced the Red Sea. A miracle then happened, as God **S**PLIT the sea and the Jews walked through it to their freedom.

The main mitzvah of the night is to:
TELL OF THE EXODUS FROM EGYPT

Page 19

TEN PLAGUES

1. Blood
2. Frogs
3. Lice
4. Wild beasts
5. Cattle sickness
6. Boils
7. Hail
8. Locust
9. Darkness
10. Death of the first-born

Page 20 and 21

1. Pesach
   homes
2. Matzah
   Egypt
   bread
   Matzah
3. Maror
   Egypt
   slaves

Page 24 and 25

wash
matzah / eat
dip / bitter herbs / charoset / eat
matzah / maror

Page 26 and 27

On Passover we do not eat Chametz. Chametz is **food made with leavening. Leavening is what makes food rise or expand.**

Not chametz: **chicken; apples; potato chips; pickles; chocolate; tomato soup.**

ANSWER: <u>A F I K O M A N</u>

Page 33

1. *Kadeish*
2. *Urchatz*
3. *Karpas*
4. *Yachatz*
5. *Maggid*
6. *Rachtzah*
7. *Motzi Matzah*
8. *Maror*
9. *Koreich*
10. *Shulchan Oreich*
11. *Tzafun*
12. *Bareich*
13. *Hallel*
14. *Nirtzah*

Glossary

afikoman—A piece of matzah that is broken off and hidden. The meal cannot be concluded until the *afikoman* is found and eaten.

Bareich—Step twelve: saying the blessing after the meal.

beitzah—Hebrew for egg.

chametz—Leavening, or food containing leavening, which is prohibited during Passover.

charoset—Mixture of fruits, nuts, and wine. The common Ashkenazi version is made with apples, walnuts, cinnamon, and wine. Versions from other parts of the world are made with dried fruits and ingredients as varied as orange blossom syrup, poppy seeds, or coconut.

chazeret—Additional *maror* to be used in the *Korech* sandwich, generally romaine lettuce or endive.

Haggadah—Book used at the seder, containing liturgy, songs, and readings.

Hallel—Step thirteen: reciting songs of praise.

k'arah—Seder plate. Some seder plates have room for five items, some for six.

Kadeish—Step one: blessing over the first cup of wine.

karpas—Parsley. Also, step three: dipping the parsley in salt water.

Korech—Step nine: combining matzah and *maror* together to make a "Hillel sandwich."

Maggid—Step five: the telling of the story of Passover, including the Four Questions and the recounting of the Ten Plagues.

maror—Bitter herbs, commonly romaine lettuce or horseradish. Also, step eight: dipping bitter herbs in the *charoset,* reciting the blessing over the bitter herbs, and eating them.

matzah—Special unleavened bread eaten on Passover. Plural: matzot.

Motzi Matzah—Step seven: reciting the blessing over food, then the blessing over matzah, and eating the matzah.

Nirtzah—Step fourteen: the conclusion of the seder, at which we say, "Next year in Jerusalem!"

Rachtzah—Step six: ritual washing of the hands.

seder—Festive Passover meal.

Shulchan Oreich—Step ten: enjoying the festive meal.

Tzafun—Step eleven: eating the *afikoman.*

Urchatz—Step two: washing the hands.

Yachatz—Step four: breaking of the middle matzah.

z'roa—shank bone.

Further UAHC Resources on Passover

Burstein, Chaya M. *The UAHC Kids Catalog of Jewish Living*. 1992.
Living as a Jew doesn't just happen. It take some doing. This book for children addresses the question "doing what?" Through puzzles, activities, biographical profiles and stories, this book provides a liberal perspective for children about Jewish living, including a section on celebrating Jewish holidays.

Heymsfeld, Carla. *The Matzah Ball Fairy*. Illustrated by Vlad Guzner. 1996.
This beautifully illustrated, full-color book is a whimsical look at one family's hilarious Passover happenings.

Koffsky, Ann. *My Jewish Holiday Fun Book*. 2000.
This activity book is chock-full of projects and information about Jewish holidays for children. Several of the activities focus on Passover fun.

Kress, Camille. *Tree Trunk Seder*. 2000.
Board books are a wonderful way to introduce young children to the joys of Judaism. This lavishly illustrated board book chronicles the celebration of Passover at the home of a family of squirrels in the woods.

Kukoff, Lydia, and Stephen J. Einstein. *Introduction to Judaism: A Sourcebook*. 1999.
A useful source book on both Jewish holidays and life cycle events for adults, this book contains a wealth of information on Passover.

Rauchwerger, Lisa. *Chocolate Chip Challah and Other Twists on the Jewish Holiday Table*: *An Interactive Family Cookbook*. 1999.
Food is central to the celebration of Passover. This delicious and humorous illustrated cookbook, designed to allow families to cook together, contains many wonderful recipes for Passover.

Syme, Daniel. *The Jewish Home*. 1988.
Each Jewish holiday and life cycle event are explained in this basic reference book for adults.

Wylen, Stephen M. *Book of the Jewish Year*. 1996.
This full-color book for children includes information, stories and background for each Jewish holiday.

Books are available from

UAHC Press
888-489-UAHC
www.uahcpress.com